The INSIDE & OUT GUIDE to
SPACECRAFT

CLARE HIBBERT

THE INSIDE AND OUT GUIDE TO SPACECRAFT
was produced by

David West 👫 **Children's Books**
7 Princeton Court
55 Felsham Road
London SW15 1AZ

Designer: Gary Jeffrey
Illustrator: Alex Pang
Editor: Dominique Crowley
Consultant: Dr Iain M. Martin
Picture Research: Victoria Cook

First published in Great Britain by Heinemann
Library, Halley Court, Jordan Hill, Oxford
OX2 8EJ, part of Harcourt Education.
Heinemann is a registered trademark
of Harcourt Education Ltd.

11 10 09 08 07 06
10 9 8 7 6 5 4 3 2 1

10 digit ISBN: 0 431 18308 2 (hardback)
13 digit ISBN: 978 0 431 18308 4
10 digit ISBN: 0 431 18315 5 (paperback)
13 digit ISBN: 978 0 431 18315 2

British Library Cataloguing in Publication Data

Hibbert, Clare
    Spacecraft. - (The inside & out guides)
    1. Space vehicles - Juvenile literature
    I. Title
    629.4'7

Printed and bound in China

PHOTO CREDITS :
Abbreviations: t-top, m-middle, b-bottom, r-right,
l-left, c-centre.

All images courtesy of NASA except page 27t, EAA photo,
27m, copyright Mojave Space Ventures Inc. photograph by
David Moore. SpaceShipOne is a Paul G Allen project.

Every effort has been made to contact copyright
holders of any material reproduced in this book.
Any omissions will be rectified in subsequent
printings if notice is given to the publishers.

*An explanation of difficult words can be
found in the glossary on pages 30 and 31.*

The INSIDE & OUT GUIDE to
SPACECRAFT

CLARE HIBBERT

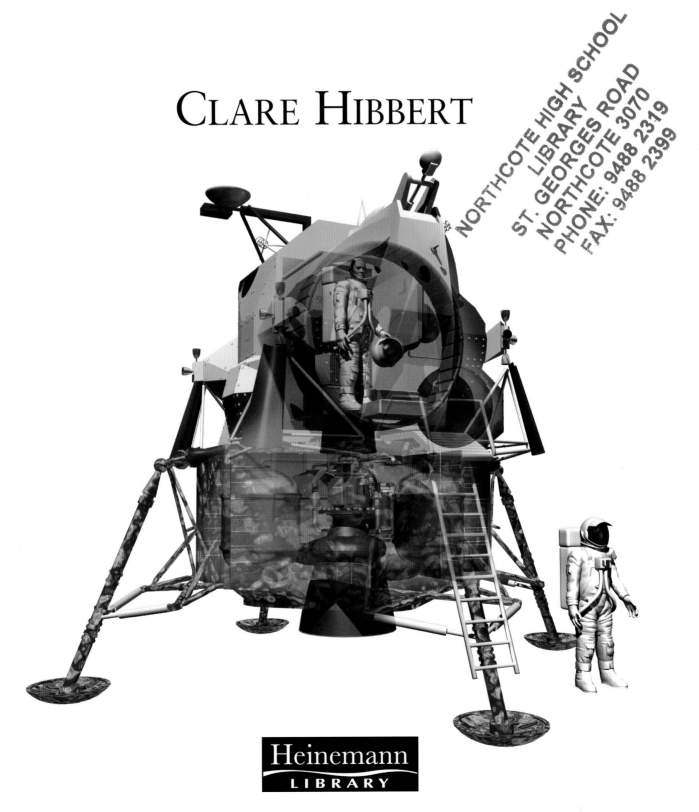

Heinemann
LIBRARY

CONTENTS

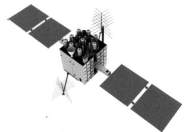

INTRODUCTION

than a dream. In the 1950s, the USA and **Soviet Union** began to adapt rockets – first developed for firing missiles – so that they could launch **spacecraft**. So far, manned space missions have stopped at the Moon, but robot **probes** have travelled beyond our Solar System and space telescopes can show us the distant edges of the Universe. Satellites, and other spacecraft technology, have changed life on Earth forever, too.

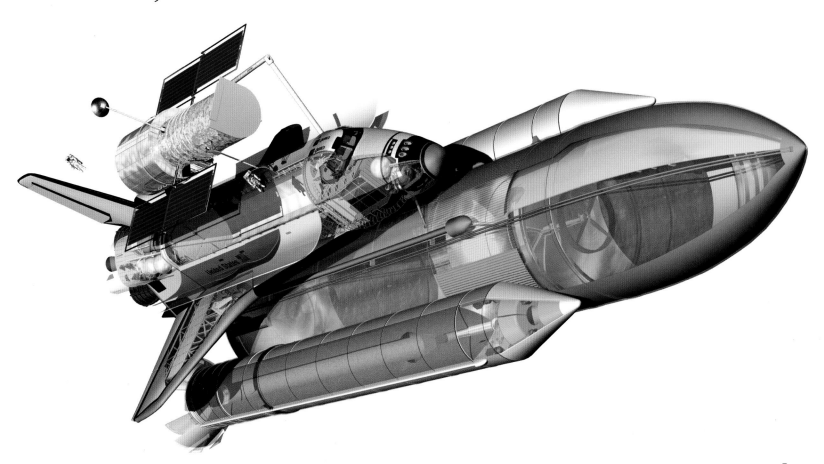

EARLY SPACECRAFT

IN OCTOBER 1957, THE SOVIETS PUT THE FIRST SATELLITE, *Sputnik 1*, into orbit. Soon afterwards, the United States and Soviet Union began the race to blast a person into space.

Both sides carried out test flights – unmanned or carrying animals – in preparation for human spaceflight. The Soviet spacecraft *Sputnik 5* took two dogs, two rats, 40 mice, and some fruit flies into space and back! *Sputnik 10* was the first human mission. **Cosmonaut** Yuri Gagarin **orbited** (travelled around) the Earth once. Three weeks later, Alan Shepard became the first American in space, though he did not orbit Earth.

VOSTOK ROCKET

Like most rockets, *Vostok* had several **stages**. Within five minutes, every stage except the final one had burned all its fuel and fallen away.

Capsule

Rocket

Gas storage bottles

Cosmonaut

VOSTOK **RE-ENTRY CAPSULE**

The capsule carried the cosmonaut and all the instruments needed for experiments in space. Gagarin's seat **ejected** after re-entry into Earth's **atmosphere**.

Cosmonaut ejection seat

FINAL-STAGE ROCKET

The final-stage rocket burned for just over six minutes. Seconds later, it split from the capsule and fell to Earth.

Radio **antenna**

Yuri Gagarin, the first human in space, on his way to the Vostok launch pad. Behind him is his back-up, Gherman Titov. Titov made the Soviets' second manned space flight in August 1961.

MERCURY RE-ENTRY CAPSULE

There were six manned *Mercury* missions. Each had the number '7' in its name, such as *Freedom 7*, to show that all the **astronauts** had played a part.

Astronaut

Abort handle

Control panel

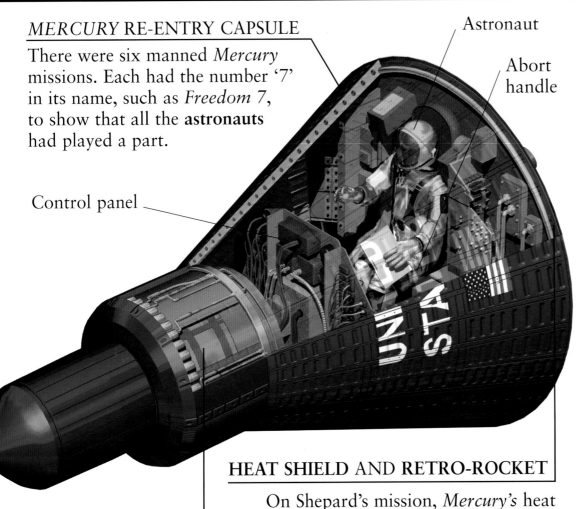

HEAT SHIELD AND RETRO-ROCKET

On Shepard's mission, *Mercury's* heat shield was made of beryllium, a metal that can take high temperatures without melting. The retro-rockets fired five minutes into the flight, to slow down the craft.

MAIN PARACHUTE

A parachute opened to slow down the capsule's descent. It opened about 4.7 km above the Earth.

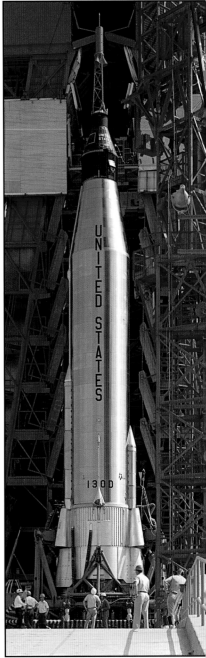

MIGHTY ATLAS
*An Atlas rocket launched the orbital Mercury missions. For **suborbital** flights, a Redstone rocket was used.*

HELLO EARTH!
On 20 February 1962 John Glenn became the first American to orbit the Earth. His mission lasted nearly five hours.

APOLLO 11

to land a man on the Moon. The *Apollo 11* mission, launched from the Kennedy Space Center, Cape Canaveral, in 1969, fulfilled that promise. For the first time in history, humans left their planet and stepped into another world.

A massive *Saturn V* rocket, the largest of the *Saturn* family, hurled the *Apollo 11* into space. The spacecraft itself was made up of two main parts, called **modules**. The command/service module (CSM) was known as *Columbia*. It flew the three crew into lunar orbit (orbit around the Moon) and then back to Earth again – a total journey of over 750,000 kilometres. The other part of the spacecraft, the lunar module (LM), carried two of the three astronauts down to the Moon's surface. In total, the mission lasted five days.

Main engine

Hydrogen tanks

SATURN V ROCKET

Saturn V stood 110 m high. It had three engine stages and a computerized instrument unit that guided the rocket during flight.

TRAVELLING TO THE MOON

During the launch, the modules were stored inside the rocket's cone-shaped nose. Once the last engine stage had separated, the command/service module turned and docked with the lunar module.

Command/service module

Lunar module

Neil Armstrong (left) was Apollo 11's commander, Michael Collins (centre) flew the command module, and Buzz Aldrin (right) flew the lunar module. All three had taken part in the Gemini missions.

SERVICE MODULE

The service module was unpressurized. It contained tanks of fuel, water, **oxygen**, and hydrogen. It separated from the command module just before re-entry.

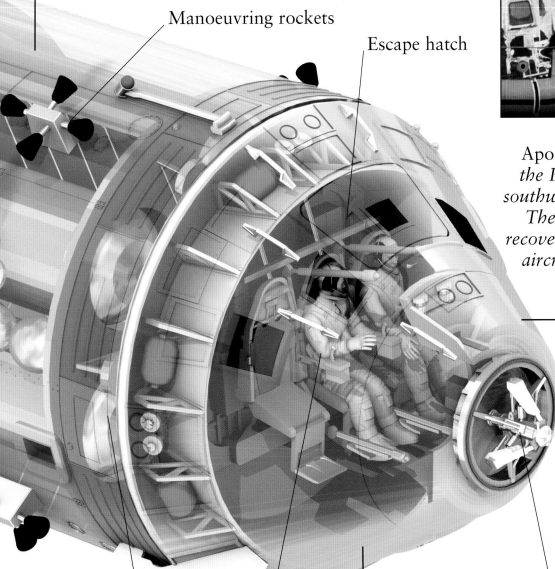

Manoeuvring rockets

Escape hatch

Astronauts

Oxygen tanks

SPLASH DOWN

Apollo 11 splashed down in the Pacific Ocean, 1,500 km southwest of Hawaii, on 24 July. The capsule and crew were recovered by a nearby American aircraft carrier, USS Hornet.

COMMAND MODULE

The front and back compartments of the command module contained the craft's engines. The inner compartment was **pressurized**. It housed the crew and the main control panels, as well as storage space for food and equipment.

Docking clamp

HEAT SHIELD

On re-entering the Earth's atmosphere, the craft reached temperatures of 3,000 °C. Its heat shield was designed to burn away, to help lose heat.

MOON LANDER

THE LUNAR MODULE (LM) WAS known as the *Eagle*. On 20 July 1969, it separated from *Columbia* and carried Armstrong and Aldrin down to the Moon. It stayed on the Moon's surface for 21 hours.

As Neil Armstrong set foot on the Moon he said, "That's one small step for a man, one giant leap for mankind." The astronauts spent over two hours outside their craft. They collected more than 20 kilograms of soil and rock samples to take back to Earth for analysis. They also planted the American flag and took a phone call from US President Richard Nixon. After climbing back into the *Eagle*, they blasted off to rejoin *Columbia* in lunar orbit. To save weight, the moon lander was left in space.

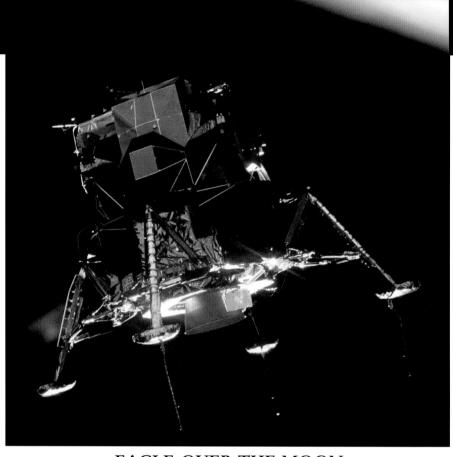

EAGLE *OVER THE MOON*
Long, thin, surface-sensing probes stick out from below Eagle's foot pads. When these detected the lunar surface, the crew cut out the engine.

MOON PRINT
Footprints created by the first astronauts are still on the Moon, as there is no wind or rain to blow or wash them away.

ALDRIN MOONWALKING
Gravity is one-sixth lighter on the Moon than it is on Earth. This creates a feeling of weightlessness, making it difficult to balance.

Mission commander Neil Armstrong had flown fighter planes for the Navy in the Korean War (1950–53). As an astronaut he made two space missions: Gemini 8 (1966) and Apollo 11.

Communications antenna

CREW COMPARTMENT

The crew compartment's tiny window allowed the men to look out on to their landing site, an area of the Moon now known as Tranquillity Base.

Reaction-control **thrusters**

ASCENT ENGINE

The ascent engine was left in lunar orbit after the crew returned to the CSM. Eventually, it crashed into the Moon.

Half-pipe to control exhaust direction

Ascent fuel tank

Entry/exit platform

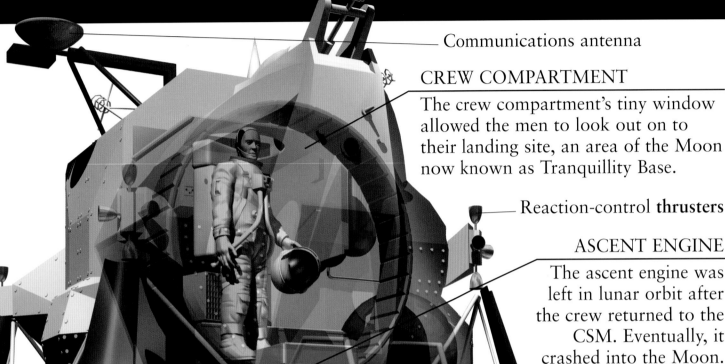

DESCENT ENGINE

When the *Eagle* landed it had less than 30 seconds' fuel left. The descent engine was left behind to lighten the load for the ascent engine.

Descent fuel tank

Foot pad

Shock absorber

MIR SPACE STATION

SPACE STATIONS allow astronauts to live and work in space for long periods. The core module of the Soviet space station *Mir* was launched in February 1986. *Mir* remained in orbit for 15 years.

The core module provided living space for up to six cosmonauts. Further modules were added in orbit: *Kvant-1* (April 1987), *Kvant-2* (December 1989), *Kristall* (June 1990), *Spektr* (May 1995), *Priroda* (April 1996), and a Shuttle docking module (November 1996). Solar panels produced some of the station's electricity; the rest came from batteries. *Mir* was continuously occupied until 1999. In 2001 it was taken out of orbit. It re-entered Earth's atmosphere near Fiji and crashed into the Pacific Ocean.

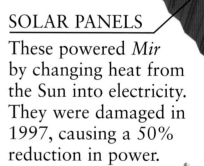

SOLAR PANELS

These powered *Mir* by changing heat from the Sun into electricity. They were damaged in 1997, causing a 50% reduction in power.

RENDEZVOUS IN SPACE
From 1995, Russia allowed US astronauts to spend time on Mir. *Space Shuttle* Atlantis *transported a Shuttle docking module to add on to* Kristall.

SOYUZ TRANSPORT SHIP

Soyuz transported cosmonauts to and from the **space station**. The *Progress* cargo spacecraft carried up supplies.

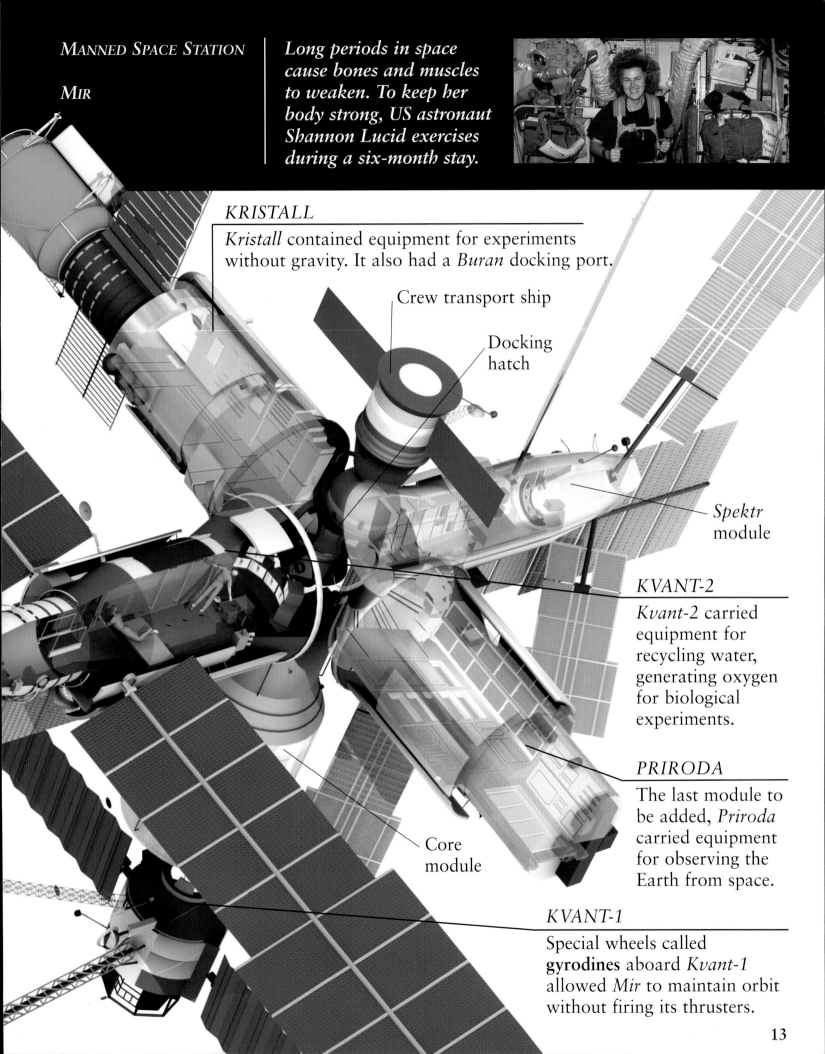

Long periods in space cause bones and muscles to weaken. To keep her body strong, US astronaut Shannon Lucid exercises during a six-month stay.

KRISTALL

Kristall contained equipment for experiments without gravity. It also had a *Buran* docking port.

Crew transport ship

Docking hatch

Spektr module

KVANT-2

Kvant-2 carried equipment for recycling water, generating oxygen for biological experiments.

PRIRODA

The last module to be added, *Priroda* carried equipment for observing the Earth from space.

Core module

KVANT-1

Special wheels called **gyrodines** aboard *Kvant-1* allowed *Mir* to maintain orbit without firing its thrusters.

13

X-PLANE

experimental rocket planes. Created purely for research, rather than for military purposes, they were built to push technology to the limit. The first X-plane, the Bell *X-1*, broke the sound barrier on 14 October 1947.

The X-plane programme was based in the Mojave Desert, California. It involved the US Air Force (USAF), NACA (the forerunner of **NASA**), and the Bell Aircraft Company. The first generation of X-planes focused on speed. Their bullet-shaped noses, thin wings, and streamlined bodies meant that air could pass over them quickly. This helped them to travel very fast. Their speed was measured in Mach numbers: Mach 1 meant the speed of sound through air, Mach 2 meant twice the speed of sound and so on.

'X' FOR EXPERIMENTAL
Early X-planes included the X-5 (top right), the first aircraft to have movable swept, or angled, wings. The XF-92A (top left) was the first aircraft with delta- or triangle-shaped wings.

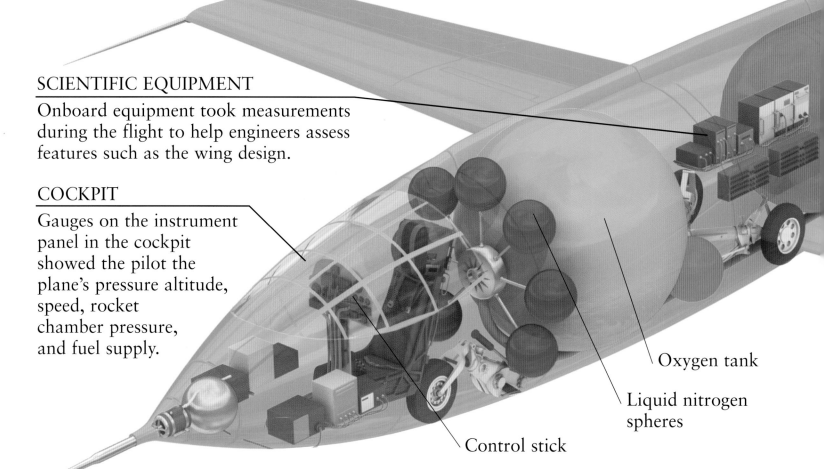

SCIENTIFIC EQUIPMENT
Onboard equipment took measurements during the flight to help engineers assess features such as the wing design.

COCKPIT
Gauges on the instrument panel in the cockpit showed the pilot the plane's pressure altitude, speed, rocket chamber pressure, and fuel supply.

Oxygen tank

Liquid nitrogen spheres

Control stick

As the test pilot of the Bell X-1, Captain Charles 'Chuck' Yeager (b. 1923) became the first human to break the sound barrier. (Sound travels through air at around 1,225 km/h.) Yeager made his name as a World War Two flying ace.

ROCKET ENGINE

The plane was powered by an *XLR-11* rocket engine that had four 2,720-kg thrust rockets.

PUSHING THE ENVELOPE
Yeager nicknamed all the planes he flew, 'Glamorous Glennis', including Bell X-1. Glennis was his wife's name.

TAILPLANE

Instead of separate **elevons**, the whole tailplane swivelled to control up and down motion.

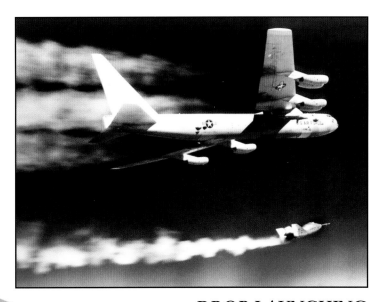

DROP LAUNCHING
In 1970, a B-52 mothership (a very large ship that carries a smaller one) launched the wingless X-24A. Experiments on the X-24s *paved the way for the Shuttle.*

FUEL TANK

The fuel tank held the plane's supply of liquid oxygen. This burned in the engine with a mix of oxygen, gas, and water.

Unswept, or straight, wing

SPACE SHUTTLE

REUSABLE SPACECRAFT BECAME A reality in 1981, when NASA carried out the test flight of its Space Transportation System (STS). Better known as the Space Shuttle, it takes off vertically, like a rocket, and lands horizontally, like an aeroplane.

The Space Shuttle is made up of an orbiter (or spaceplane), two solid-fuel rocket **boosters**, and an external fuel tank. After each flight, the orbiter returns to Earth and the rocket boosters are recovered from where they have landed in the sea. Rocket boosters can be reused for about 20 flights. The only part of the Shuttle that cannot be used again is the external fuel tank, which connects the orbiter to the rocket boosters during the launch. The Soviets' reusable spacecraft, *Buran*, made an unmanned flight in 1988, but funding cuts halted the *Buran* programme.

NICE MOVER
This picture of the Space Shuttle Discovery *was taken from the* International Space Station. *Radiators on the inside of the cargo bay doors help keep the shuttle from overheating.*

ROCKET BOOSTERS

The rocket boosters are discarded at an altitude of about 45 km. Parachutes open out behind them to slow their fall back to Earth so they can be reused.

Liquid oxygen tank

EXTERNAL FUEL TANK
The external tank carries liquid oxygen and liquid hydrogen fuel. A pipe carries this fuel to the orbiter's main engines. After all the fuel is used, the tank breaks away, and burns up in the Earth's atmosphere.

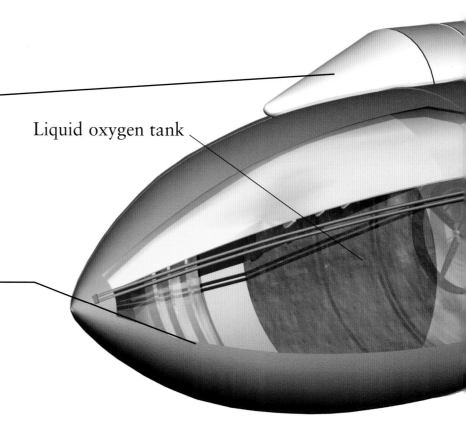

The first Space Shuttle crew were mission commander John Young (left) and pilot Bob Crippen (right). It was Crippen's first space flight, but Young's fifth. Young's most recent mission had been to the Moon, nine years earlier.

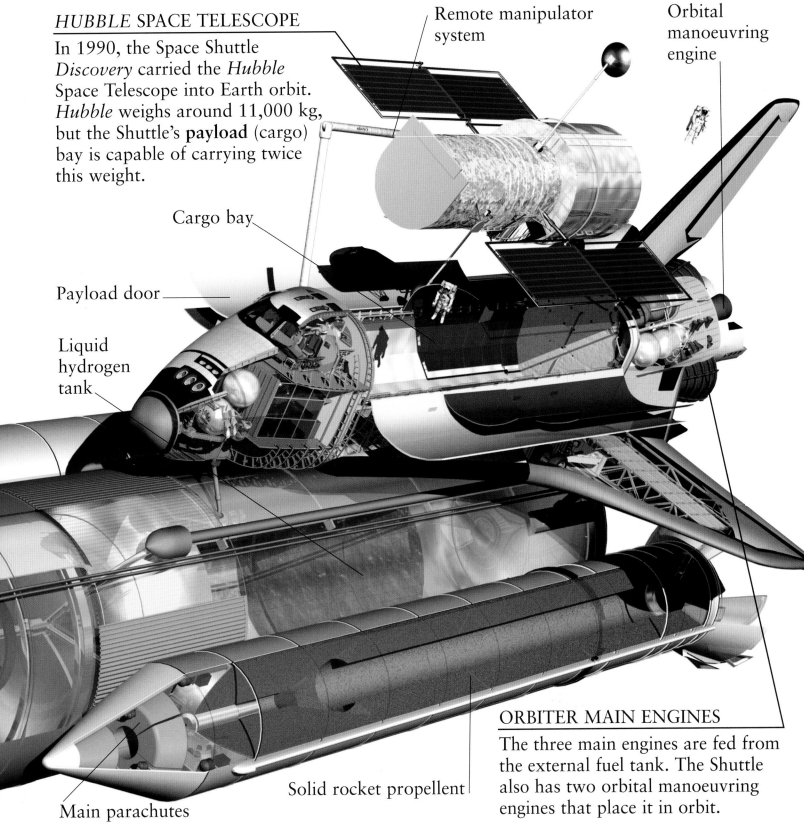

HUBBLE SPACE TELESCOPE

In 1990, the Space Shuttle *Discovery* carried the *Hubble* Space Telescope into Earth orbit. *Hubble* weighs around 11,000 kg, but the Shuttle's **payload** (cargo) bay is capable of carrying twice this weight.

Remote manipulator system

Orbital manoeuvring engine

Cargo bay

Payload door

Liquid hydrogen tank

ORBITER MAIN ENGINES

The three main engines are fed from the external fuel tank. The Shuttle also has two orbital manoeuvring engines that place it in orbit.

Solid rocket propellent

Main parachutes

SHUTTLE ORBITER

NASA HAS A FLEET of three Shuttles: *Atlantis*, *Discovery*, and *Endeavour*. Two others, *Challenger* and *Columbia*, were lost in disasters. They have flown more than 100 missions in their first 25 years of service.

The front part of the orbiter contains the living quarters and flight deck. There is space on board the Shuttle for a crew of seven. As well as carrying people into space, the Shuttle has transported satellites, space probes, and space station equipment. Most of the flights carrying parts of the *International Space Station* into orbit have been made by the Shuttle. There have also been Space Shuttle missions to repair damaged satellites.

SMOOTH LANDING
Silica tiles stop the orbiter from melting during reentry. The delta-wings help the craft to glide unpowered and a parachute slows it down. The orbiter usually lands on the 2.5 mile-long runway at the Kennedy Space Center.

LOSS OF CHALLENGER
In 1986, the Challenger *orbiter blew up during takeoff. A second disaster happened in 2003, when* Columbia *exploded during reentry. In both cases all the crew died.*

CONTROL SYSTEM

There are 44 small rocket engines at the front and back that maneuver the orbiter in space.

Eileen Collins, standing second from left, led the seven members of Space Shuttle Discovery's *crew for the 14-day mission to the* International Space Station *in August 2005.*

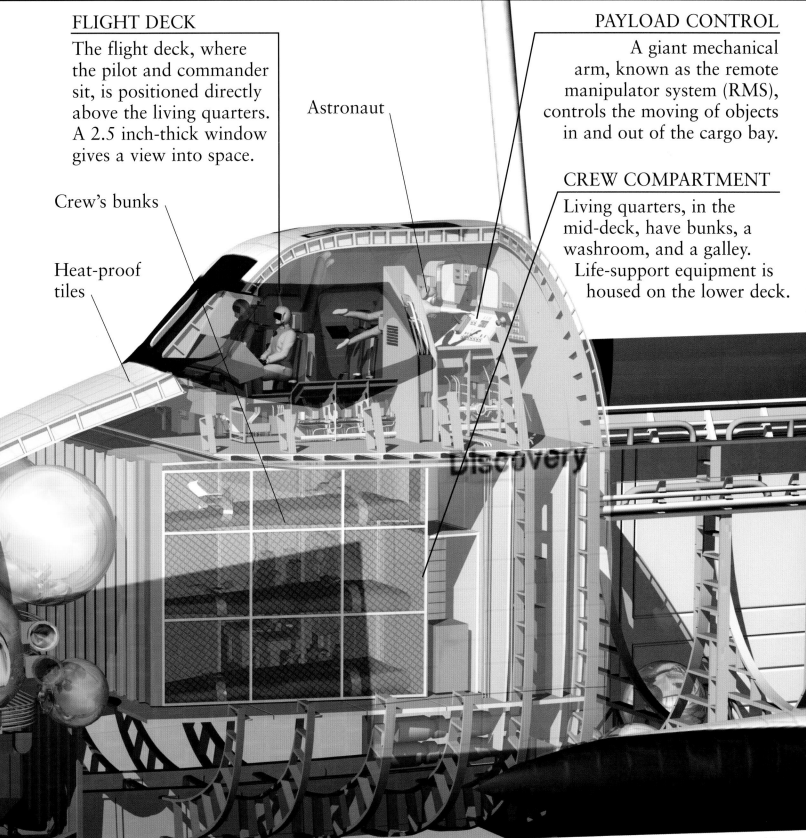

FLIGHT DECK

The flight deck, where the pilot and commander sit, is positioned directly above the living quarters. A 2.5 inch-thick window gives a view into space.

Crew's bunks

Heat-proof tiles

Astronaut

PAYLOAD CONTROL

A giant mechanical arm, known as the remote manipulator system (RMS), controls the moving of objects in and out of the cargo bay.

CREW COMPARTMENT

Living quarters, in the mid-deck, have bunks, a washroom, and a galley. Life-support equipment is housed on the lower deck.

Discovery

EVA SPACESUIT AND MMU

SPACE IS A HOSTILE ENVIRONMENT FOR A HUMAN BEING. SPACESUITS ACT AS A total life-support system during EVA (ExtraVehicular Activity) – that is, time spent outside the spacecraft.

A spacesuit is pressurized to make up for the lack of air pressure in space (without pressure, blood cannot carry oxygen to the brain). The suit also provides oxygen, shields against **radiation**, and keeps the wearer's temperature stable. It even carries away waste if the astronaut has to go to the toilet. Astronauts sometimes use a jet-powered 'chair' called an MMU (Manned Manoeuvring Unit) to fly freely in space. Before its invention, they needed a safety line so they did not float away.

BACKPACKER
In February 1984 astronaut Bruce McCandless used an MMU and took the first space 'walk' without a safety line.

RESCUE MISSION, 1984
During a six-hour EVA, astronaut Dale Gardner helped to load the Westar VI satellite on to the Shuttle to be brought to Earth for repairs.

WELL-TESTED
Astronauts practise wearing suits and MMUs under water in tanks. Floating in water is very similar to the weightless conditions in space.

20

Cosmonaut Aleksei Leonov (b. 1934) became the first person to walk in space on 18 March 1965. A camera fitted to the outside of his Voskhod 2 spacecraft recorded the historic event. His EVA lasted twelve minutes.

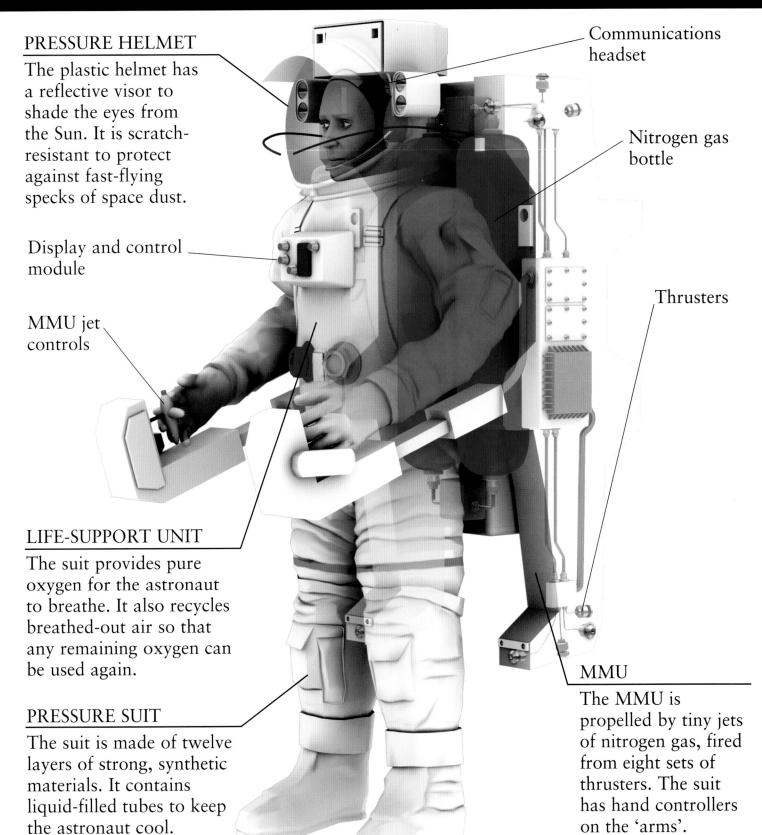

PRESSURE HELMET

The plastic helmet has a reflective visor to shade the eyes from the Sun. It is scratch-resistant to protect against fast-flying specks of space dust.

Display and control module

MMU jet controls

LIFE-SUPPORT UNIT

The suit provides pure oxygen for the astronaut to breathe. It also recycles breathed-out air so that any remaining oxygen can be used again.

PRESSURE SUIT

The suit is made of twelve layers of strong, synthetic materials. It contains liquid-filled tubes to keep the astronaut cool.

Communications headset

Nitrogen gas bottle

Thrusters

MMU

The MMU is propelled by tiny jets of nitrogen gas, fired from eight sets of thrusters. The suit has hand controllers on the 'arms'.

SATELLITE

A SATELLITE IS SOMETHING that orbits Earth (or another body in space). Earth has one natural satellite—the Moon—and about 3,000 currently active artificial satellites.

Artificial orbiters include space telescopes, weather satellites, and spy satellites. Comsats (communications satellites) transmit TV programs and telephone calls in the form of radio signals. They contain a device, called a transponder, that cleans up and strengthens the signals. Comsats in high orbit move at the same speed as Earth and remain in constant contact with their control center. Satellites in lower orbits may only make contact with ground control every ten minutes.

SOLAR PANEL
The satellite adjusts the position of its solar panels, so that they are always facing the Sun. The panels collect energy from the Sun and turn it into electricity.

WEATHER OBSERVING SATELLITE
This new satellite helps scientists to predict the weather accurately, as well as aiding U.S. search and rescue missions. It reached orbit on May 20, 2005.

TEST INFLATION OF ECHO 1
NASA launched two Echo communications satellites in the 1960s. They were shiny silver globes able to bounce back radio waves. They could be seen in the sky from Earth.

A Soviet technician puts the finishing touches to Sputnik 1, *which was the first artificial satellite in space.* Sputnik *successfully launched into Earth orbit on October 4, 1957.*

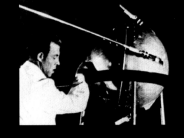

Satellite platform

ANTENNA
The antenna sends focused beams of radio signals to the receiving dish of a ground station on Earth.

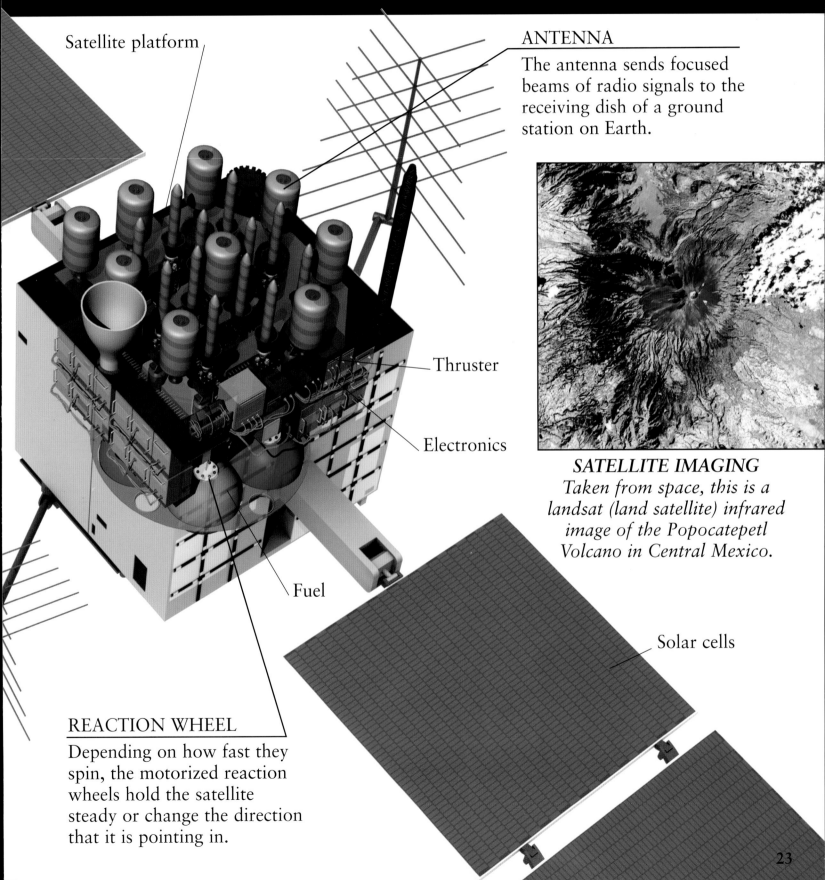

Thruster

Electronics

SATELLITE IMAGING
Taken from space, this is a landsat (land satellite) infrared image of the Popocatepetl Volcano in Central Mexico.

Fuel

Solar cells

REACTION WHEEL
Depending on how fast they spin, the motorized reaction wheels hold the satellite steady or change the direction that it is pointing in.

MARS PATHFINDER

THE 1997 *PATHFINDER* mission placed the first robot explorer, *Sojourner*, on Mars. The mission was also able to find out more about the Martian surface and atmosphere.

The *Pathfinder* **lander** had three metal solar panels that opened out like petals after landing. *Pathfinder* was part of a new wave of exploration. *Mars Global Surveyor* began to orbit Mars in 1997. By 2001, it had mapped the entire surface. In January 2004, the twin Mars Exploration Rovers (MERs), *Spirit* and *Opportunity*, landed at separate Martian sites, one of which may once have been a lake. Part of their mission was to search for any evidence of water.

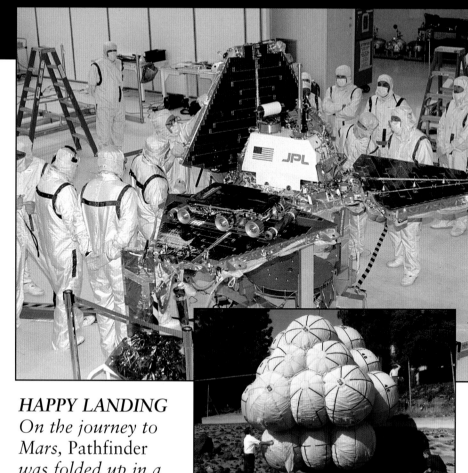

HAPPY LANDING
On the journey to Mars, Pathfinder *was folded up in a pyramid shape with* Sojouner *inside. About 100 m above the Martian surface, 24 airbags inflated to cushion the landing.*

LIFE ON MARS?
Landers and orbiters have sent back images that suggest Mars once had water. The area in this photograph could have been a flood site. If there was water, perhaps there was life too.

In 1976, the US space probes Viking 1 *and 2 landed on Mars and sent back the first close-up pictures of the planet's surface. They also carried out tests on its soil, monitored the weather, and tested the atmosphere.*

PANORAMIC CAMERA

Spirit's panoramic camera is fixed to a 1.5m-high mast. It can take high-resolution, 360-degree images that show Mars as if through human eyes.

SOLAR PANELS

In March 2005 *Spirit's* solar panels suddenly became more efficient. A storm probably blew off its build-up of dust!

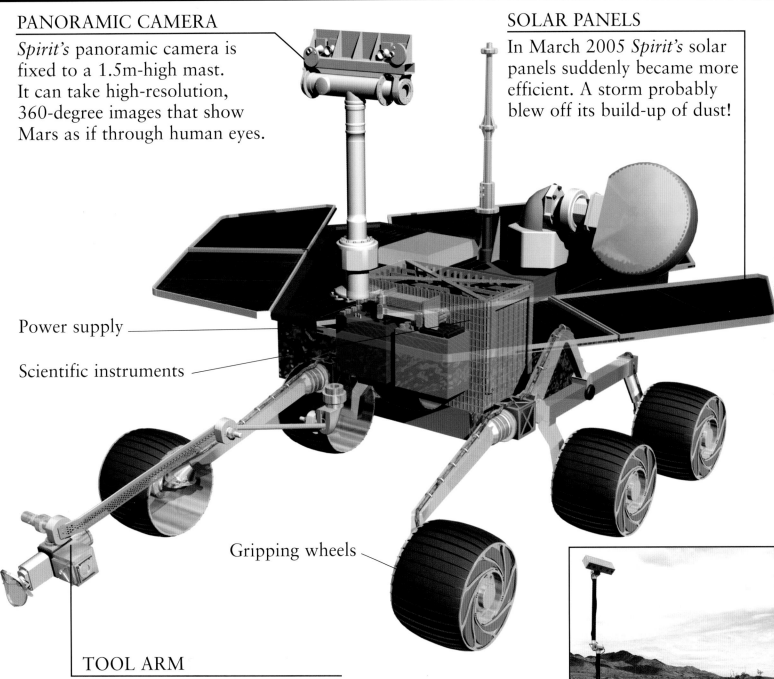

Power supply

Scientific instruments

Gripping wheels

TOOL ARM

Spirit carries equipment for testing rocks, magnets for collecting magnetic dust particles, a microscopic camera for taking close-up images, and a rock hammer for producing samples to study.

ROBUST ROBOT

Sojourner *was the size of a microwave oven. It had to keep its balance on the rocky terrain as it crawled along at 60 cm per minute.*

SPACESHIPONE

spacecraft had been part of a government-funded program. That changed with the first crewed flight of *SpaceShipOne*, a rocket plane built by a private company, Scaled Composites, based in California and funded solely by Microsoft founder Paul G. Allen.

Like the X-planes, *SpaceShipOne* is designed to be drop-launched from a mothership, but it can land by itself. After launch the plane fires its rocket engine for an 80-second burn and shoots up through the atmosphere to a height of 62 miles (where space begins). *SpaceShipOne* reaches speeds of Mach 3.5 during its climb. At around 62 miles, the plane adjusts its wings to make a "feather" shape, which helps it to slow down by catching air. Then it reenters the atmosphere and plummets toward Earth. About 12 miles above the ground it changes back to a glider shape for landing.

PRESSURIZED FUSELAGE

No one has to wear a spacesuit or breathing mask in SpaceShipOne because the cabin is pressurized and has oxygen piped into it. There is also a system to take away carbon dioxide and any moisture in the air.

FLIGHT CONTROLS

The pilot has manual controls for steering and navigation. The plane also has an onboard computer with direct radio links to mission control on the ground.

SUPERSTRONG SKIN

SpaceShipOne is strong but extremely light. Its body is made of a mixture of graphite and epoxy resin. Parts that heat up the most, such as the fronts of the wings, have a heat-proof coating.

Viewing port, or window

Burt Rutan (b. 1943) is a test pilot and aircraft designer. In 1984 he set up Scaled Composites, the company that developed SpaceShipOne. Rutan made his name with the design of the Voyager (1986), the first plane to fly non-stop around the world without refuelling.

LAUNCH CRAFT

With SpaceShipOne tucked under its body, the mothership White Knight takes about an hour to climb 9 miles. From this height it launches the rocket plane. White Knight is powered by twin turbojets.

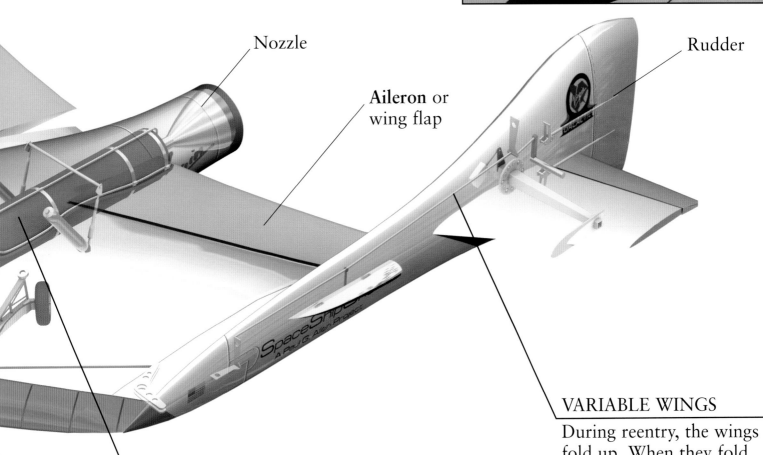

Nozzle

Aileron or wing flap

Rudder

VARIABLE WINGS

During reentry, the wings fold up. When they fold down, the spaceplane changes to a glider shape, which helps it to fly through the air.

HYBRID ROCKET MOTOR

The rocket burns a mix of nitrous oxide (laughing gas) and rubber. It is called a hybrid because it copies features from both solid- and liquid-fuel rockets.

ISS

yet. Like previous space stations, the *ISS* is made up of modules that fit together. What is different is that these modules have come from a team of different countries.

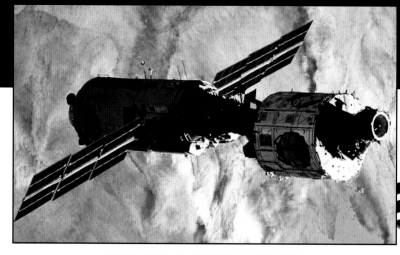

The USA has contributed most to the *ISS*; other nations involved include Russia, Japan, Canada, and ten European Space Agency (ESA) countries. Assembling the space station is a massive task. The first steps were taken in December 1998, when a Russian power processor called *Zarya* was connected to a US node called *Unity*. (A node is a connector that links other modules.) In total, the *ISS* has more than 100 parts, which build into nodes, solar panels, living quarters, and laboratories. The space station should be complete by 2009.

HUMBLE BEGINNINGS
In 1998, the Zarya *power unit (top, with solar wings) connected to the* Unity *node. The first parts of the* ISS *were operational at last.*

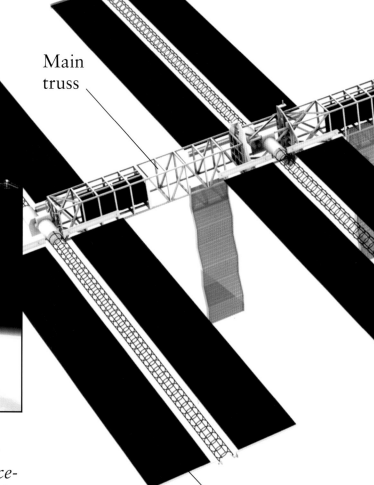

Main truss

Solar arrays

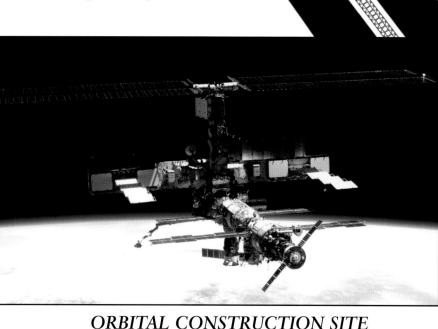

ORBITAL CONSTRUCTION SITE
The ISS is in low orbit, about 360 km above the Earth. Robot arms join the various parts, then space-walking astronauts complete the assembly by hand.

Marcos Pontes (left) of Brazil, Pavel Vinogradov of Russia (centre), and Jeffrey Williams of NASA (right) joined the ISS crew in March 2006.

Zenith truss

Main truss

Zvezda service module

Zarya

Unity

Thermal panel

KIBO JEM

Kibo is the Japanese Experiment Module (JEM). This lab is for experiments in zero-gravity.

Robot arm

Oxygen tanks

Space Shuttle

DESTINY LAB

Destiny houses a laboratory and the *ISS*'s control centre.

COLUMBUS MODULE

The European laboratory *Columbus* is scheduled for launch by the Shuttle in 2007.

SOLAR ARRAYS

The *ISS* needs lots of electrical power. It has about 4,000 sq m of solar cells that change sunlight into electricity.

HOME SWEET HOME

Russia provided the first living quarters, to hold two people. A second US module will take the crew capacity up to seven. Oxygen is stored in large tanks (shown here in green).

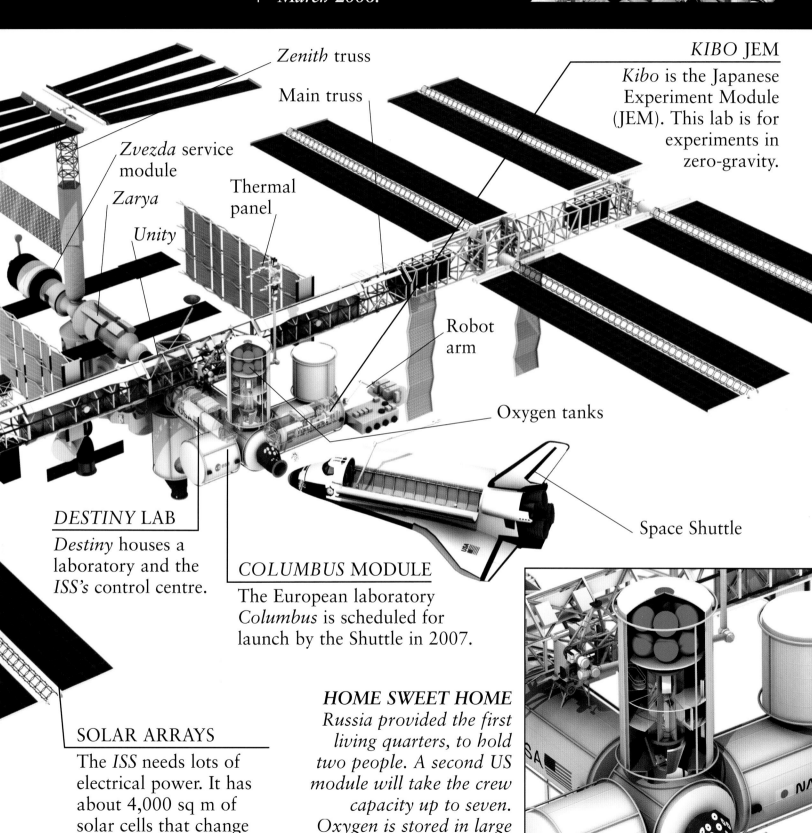

GLOSSARY

aileron
Wing flap that gives balance

antenna
Device that can pick up radio or electrical signals

astronaut
Someone who is trained to fly into space. The word means "star-sailor."

atmosphere
Blanket of air that surrounds Earth. It stops at about 62 miles and that is where space begins.

booster
Extra rocket that provides more power for the launch of a rocket or Space Shuttle

capsule
Small spacecraft

cosmonaut
Soviet or Russian word for someone who is trained to fly into space. The word means "sailor of the universe."

docking
When two spacecraft join together in space

ejected
To be thrown out

elevon
Surface on an airplane that controls rolling, diving, and climbing

gravity
Force that pulls everything down to the ground and keeps satellites orbiting Earth and planets orbiting the Sun

heat shield
Coating on the outside of a spacecraft to protect it from high temperatures

hydrogen
Light gas with no taste or smell that burns quickly in air

lander
Spacecraft designed to land on the surface of another world

launch pad
Platform from which a rocket or Space Shuttle takes off

module
A smaller part that fits into other parts to make something bigger

NASA
Short for National Aeronautics and Space Administration. The U.S. government organization in charge of the United States' space program.

orbit
Circular path around a body in space

oxygen
Gas found in Earth's atmosphere that all animals, including humans, need to breathe in order to stay alive

payload
Load or cargo that a rocket carries into space, for example a satellite or space probe

pressurized
Having normal atmospheric pressure, like on Earth

probe
Unmanned spacecraft

radiation
Rays of energy, such as the heat and light energy, given off by the Sun

reentry
Coming back into Earth's atmosphere from space

retro-rocket
Small rocket that fires in the opposite direction to slow down a spacecraft

Soviet Union
Collection of communist republics, led by Russia, that broke up in 1991

spacecraft
Any vehicle that travels into space, manned or unmanned

space station
Large, manned spacecraft that stays in space for many years

splash down
Landing a spacecraft in the ocean

stage
Part of a rocket

suborbital
Flight shorter than a full orbit

tailplane
Small, horizontal wing at the back of an aircraft

thruster
Small rocket engine that fires up to help a spacecraft change direction

truss
Supportive structure

INDEX

DATE DUE

RAECO